Massacre at Camp Grant

T0163466

MASSACRE at CAMP GRANT

Forgetting and Remembering Apache History

CHIP COLWELL-CHANTHAPHONH

The University of Arizona Press   Tucson

 THE UNIVERSITY OF
ARIZONA PRESS

www.uapress.arizona.edu

Library of Congress Cataloging-in-Publication Data
Colwell-Chanthaphonh, Chip (John Stephen), 1975–
Massacre at Camp Grant : forgetting and remembering Apache history
/ Chip Colwell-Chanthaphonh.
p. cm.
Includes bibliographical references and index.
ISBN 978-0-8165-2585-0 (pbk. : alk. paper)
1. Apache Indians—Wars. 2. Apache Indians—History—19th century.
3. Massacres—Arizona—Aravaipa Canyon. 4. Indians of North
America—Crimes against—Arizona—Aravaipa Canyon. 5. Indians,
Treatment of—Arizona—Aravaipa Canyon. 6. Aravaipa Canyon
(Ariz.)—History. I. Title.
E99.A6C595   2007
973.8'2–dc22   2006032952

An earlier version of chapter 2 was published in the American Indian
Quarterly, volume 27, numbers 3 & 4, copyright © 2004 by the Univer-
sity of Nebraska Press; reproduced by permission of the University of
Nebraska Press. Chapter 4 has been adapted from "The 'Camp Grant
Massacre' in the Historical Imagination," published in the Journal of
the Southwest 45, no. 3 (Autumn 2003): 349–369.

Publication of this book is made possible in part by a publication
grant from the Charles Redd Center for Western Studies at Brigham
Young University.

The royalties for this book have been donated to the San Carlos
Apache Elders Cultural Advisory Council.

Manufactured in the United States of America on acid-free, archival
quality paper and processed chlorine free.

16   15   14   13   12   6   5   4   3   2

If I were to remember other things,
I should be someone else.
—N. Scott Momaday, *The Names*